OSCAR
THE PACIFIER GNOME

This is Victor. Today is a very special day for him because he doesn't need his pacifier anymore.

So, Victor asked his mommy to Write a letter to the pacifier gnome.

This is Oscar, the pacifier gnome. He works as Santa's Helper at the recycling department changing old pacifiers into new toys.

Do you know what recycling means? It means changing old materials into new ones, so they can be reused.

Glass bottles

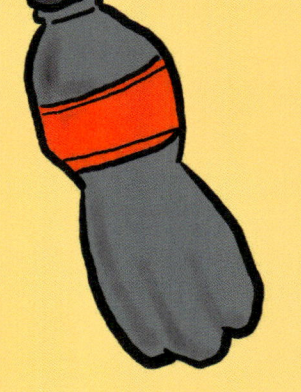

Cans

Plastic bottles

Newspapers and magazines

Oscar has just received a new letter. He will soon go for another visit. This time to Victor's house.

As soon as dusk goes down, Oscar goes on to make another delivery.

Oscar always makes his deliveries by bike because besides being a great exercise it does not pollute the atmosphere.

Before he goes to bed, Victor looks at his pacifier for the last time.

During the night Oscar enters Victor's room through the window, gets his pacifier and leaves a surprise gift in its place.

As soon as Victor wakes up, he discovers the gift beside his bed.

He rushes to his mommy to show her the new gift.

The next day
Victor told his
classmates
about Oscar, the
pacifier gnome
and how important
recycling is to the
world.

Printed in Great Britain
by Amazon